The
FOCUS
of
PRAYER

A balanced prayer life

IAN FALLIS

NEW TRIBES MISSION

ISBN:
978-0-9968348-0-3

Table of Contents

Author's Foreword

I'd like to think that discovering an important yet overlooked fact about prayer would change a person's life.

Unfortunately, it does not.

Years ago, I learned something significant about prayer. But when I started to write this book, it was truly ironic that I was writing about prayer. I had the third-worst prayer life of any Christian in the Western Hemisphere. (It's true—I took a quiz on Facebook.)

So writing this book was a great fit for me, for two reasons.

First, this was the perfect place for a writer to be. I had no qualifications to say to you, "Here is the right way." I couldn't set myself up as an example. I could only let God be God. I could only point to what I've seen in His Word and, with wonder and excitement, say, "Hey, come over here! Look what I found!"

Second, working through this book allowed me to apply that fact to my prayer life. And it helped. Tremendously. Facts don't change people. God changes people. God frequently uses prayer to reorient our hearts toward Him, and that's when change begins.

So here's my invitation to join me as, together, we explore and pray through what God says about prayer. I'll show you what God used to change my prayers, and thus, my life. Let's find joy on this journey …

Ian Fallis

Praying for self | Praying for believers | Praying with God

The Setup

Day 1: Capturing light

Ever tried to capture light?

You probably have. That's what photography is, and it's everywhere these days. Instagram, Pinterest, Flickr and more are built around photos. You probably have a camera everywhere you go, in your pocket or purse. It seems as if everyone does.

Let's compare photography and prayer.

Good photos balance three elements essential to capturing light. The size of the hole the light comes through influences how much of the photo appears to be in focus. The length of time the light is allowed to come through the hole can "freeze" an image or blur it. The light sensitivity of the material the light falls on determines whether an image is "grainy" or fine.

Balancing these three elements brings out a depth, breadth and richness that are missing in so much point-and-shoot photography.

As with photography, there's depth, breadth and richness to be found in prayers that are balanced according to what we find in Scripture. That's what this book is about. Welcome to the journey.

Let's start with praying for …

- God to focus our thoughts on prayer;
- A heart that is sensitive to God; and
- The ability and the will to put time and effort into balancing our prayers.

Next, we'll see what we can do about selfies in our prayer lives.

Praying for self | Praying for believers | Praying with God

Study Guide, Day 1

Prayer is you and me, with our flaws and shortcomings, having a conversation with the eternal, perfect, infinite Creator. Think about that in light of what God says in Isaiah 55:8-9:

"For My thoughts are not your thoughts, nor are your ways My ways," says the LORD. "For as the heavens are higher than the earth, so are My ways higher than your ways, and My thoughts than your thoughts."

What bearing should that passage have on how you think about and approach prayer?

_____

_____

_____

_____

_____

_____

_____

And yet this same God tells us in Hebrews 4:16 to come to him with confidence:

Let us therefore come boldly to the throne of grace, that we may obtain mercy and find grace to help in time of need.

5

What does it say to you that the Creator wants you to come to Him boldly?

_____

_____

_____

_____

_____

_____

_____

We live in a point-and-shoot age, and I'm not just talking about photography. Sometimes our prayers could be characterized as point-and-shoot. That's OK—we're still praying, pointed toward God, and taking our concerns to Him. But do you think you can find more depth and richness in your prayer life? Try to put into words how you want your prayer life to change.

_____

_____

_____

_____

_____

Week 1

Praying for yourself

Ian Fallis

Praying for self | Praying for believers | Praying with God

Day 2: All about selfies

Hear my prayer, O LORD, and give ear to my cry; do not be silent at my tears; for I am a stranger with You, a sojourner, as all my fathers were. Remove Your gaze from me, that I may regain strength, before I go away and am no more. Psalm 39:12-14

If selfies are so awful, why do we keep taking them?

The truth is, it's not always wrong to focus on yourself, whether we're talking about photographs or prayer. A quick glance at the Psalms makes that obvious. David, a man after God's own heart, frequently painted word pictures of his circumstances and prayed about the situations he found himself in.

And let's be honest: Sometimes it seems like he was being whiny.

So it's perfectly normal to focus on yourself when you pray. No one else has your perspective on your circumstances. No one else really knows how you feeling and what you're experiencing. You can bring those to God in a way that no one else can.

It's definitely a problem if we never see beyond ourselves, and we'll spend time on that later. But first, let's look at how we can be most effective in praying for ourselves.

So take a moment to gather your thoughts. What is it about your life that you would like to see change? What do you want to be different? Let's not worry about the solutions right now. Simply bring your concerns to God. Quiet your mind and speak to the Lord on your own behalf.

Praying for self | Praying for believers | Praying with God

Study Guide, Day 2

Take a few minutes to jot down your thoughts about the situation or situations in your life that you brought before God.

_____

_____

_____

_____

_____

Read Romans 8:18-39, and pay particular attention to verses 38 and 39: *For I am persuaded that neither death nor life, nor angels nor principalities nor powers, nor things present nor things to come, nor height nor depth, nor any other created thing, shall be able to separate us from the love of God which is in Christ Jesus our Lord.*

What assurances do you see that God knows what you're going through? What do you see that says God cares?

_____

_____

_____

_____

_____

_____

Why should this make you feel confident about
bringing your situation to God?

_____

_____

_____

_____

_____

Praying for self | Praying for believers | Praying with God

Day 3: Let's be honest

How long, O LORD? Will You forget me forever?
How long will You hide Your face from me? How
long shall I take counsel in my soul, having sorrow
in my heart daily? How long will my enemy be
exalted over me? Psalm 13:1-2

Do you ever get angry with God? Does it
ever seem like He's not listening? Do you get
discouraged?

David certainly did.

The big difference between us and David is
what he did with those feelings. Maybe at first
he bottled them up, or he grumbled to himself.
But whether he did or not, he let God know
what he was thinking and how he was feeling.
And he didn't hold back.

Picture yourself speaking to God that way:

"Hey, Father, have You forgotten about
me? Are You hiding from me? Have You not
noticed that I'm crying myself to sleep each
and every night? Are You just going to let this
drag on and on? Don't You care?"

How would you feel about saying that to
God?

The thing is, we sometimes think that way, but we hesitate to say that to God. Why? He knows exactly what we're thinking. And more important, He cares about us. He loves us unconditionally.

It makes a lot of sense to simply be honest with God.

Tell Him how you're feeling. Let Him know what you're thinking. Lay it all out there. He prefers it that way. How do we know He wants to hear our raw feelings and fears? Because He had David write out his own struggles for us to see and to learn from.

Study Guide, Day 3

For thirty-six chapters of Job (Job 2-37), Job's friends ramble, and Job expresses questions and doubts. Finally God answers Job (Job 38:1) for two chapters. After two sentences from Job (Job 40:3-5), God speaks for two more chapters, leading to this in Job 42:1-7 and 12:

Then Job answered the LORD and said: "I know that You can do everything, and that no purpose of Yours can be withheld from You. You asked, 'Who is this who hides counsel without knowledge?' Therefore I have uttered what I did not understand, things too wonderful for me, which I did not know.

"Listen, please, and let me speak; You said, 'I will question you, and you shall answer Me.' I have heard of You by the hearing of the ear, but now my eye sees You. Therefore I abhor myself, and repent in dust and ashes."

And so it was, after the LORD had spoken these words to Job, that the LORD said to Eliphaz the Temanite, "My wrath is aroused against you and your two friends, for you have not spoken of Me what is right, as My servant Job has."… Now the LORD blessed the latter days of Job more than his beginning.

What could Job complain to God about? (Job 1:13-18) What was Job's response? Was it appropriate? (Job 1:20-22)

_____

_____

_____

_____

_____

God was silent from Job 2 through Job 37. And after He spoke, Job repented and God blessed him. What does this say about God's patience? What does this say about His forgiveness? What does it say about His love? Why did Job repent?

_____

_____

_____

_____

Does this seem like a God you can be honest with? Why or why not?

_____

_____

_____

_____

_____

Day 4: Time to listen

Consider and hear me, O LORD my God; enlighten
my eyes, lest I sleep the sleep of death; lest my
enemy say, "I have prevailed against him"; lest
those who trouble me rejoice when I am moved.
Psalm 13:3-4

If it feels awkward to speak to God the
way David did, it's even more challenging to
say, "enlighten my eyes." David is asking God
to show him the situation as God sees it.

That's often the missing ingredient when
we're feeling downtrodden, discouraged and
damaged. And that's one of the benefits of
prayer. We can let all of that out. We can
honestly tell God how we're feeling and what
we're thinking. We can even come right out
and say, "This is all Your fault!"

And then it's time to ask Him to enlighten
our eyes, and be still and listen.

That may sound odd. You may think,
"God doesn't talk to me." You may even think,
"Wow, this guy thinks God speaks to him. He
must be crazy." Maybe, but not in this case.
Jesus said, "He who is of God hears God's
words" (John 8:47), and "My sheep hear My

voice" (John 10:27). God's Word not only tells us to listen to Him, it's evidence that He speaks to us.

Think about not only how He gave us the Bible, but why. We can open His Word and hear His voice whenever we want to. God desires to communicate with us, so He's made it possible for us to hear Him.

From the very beginning of the Bible, what do we see God doing? Talking with Adam and Eve. After they sinned, He did not wait for them to come to Him and apologize. He went to them, and He talked with them.

OK, now I'm going to stop writing, and you're going to stop reading, and bow your head and listen expectantly for His perspective on your circumstances. Or open His Word and read prayerfully – He's always speaking to us in His Word. And you do need to compare whatever you believe you hear to His Word; He will not contradict Himself.

Praying for self | Praying for believers | Praying with God

Study Guide, Day 4

When we try to sit quietly, waiting for God, we can be our own worst enemies. The cares of the day creep in. We begin to daydream. Other noises suddenly seem quite loud—the ticking of a clock, children playing, traffic noise outside, or the buzz of a light. What steps can you take to limit distractions and make it easier for you to listen?

_____

_____

_____

_____

_____

Limiting distractions is only half the battle. You can keep your mind active and focused on God as you wait:

- Read your Bible. God often speaks to us through His Word, and the Word speaks about Him.
- Listen to music that is specifically designed to worship God.
- Focus on a nature scene and admire it as His handiwork.

- Think about times you have seen God work in your life, and thank Him and praise Him.

What are some other ways you can think of to actively listen?

_____

_____

_____

_____

_____

In 2 Timothy 3:16, we're told that *All Scripture is God-breathed and is useful for teaching, rebuking, correcting and training in righteousness.* (NIV) What does that say to you about the value of Scripture in hearing God speak?

_____

_____

_____

_____

_____

Day 5: Trust Him

But I have trusted in Your mercy; my heart shall rejoice in Your salvation. I will sing to the LORD, because He has dealt bountifully with me. Psalm 13:5-6

With his heart opened, then stilled by God, David comes back to solid ground: *"I have trusted in your mercy."* Some translations render "mercy" as love or kindness. It's the same Hebrew word the King James Version renders elsewhere as "lovingkindness," and it speaks to the relationship David had with God.

Some Bible teachers point to parallels between the lovingkindness of the Old Testament and the relationship of grace and unconditional love that believers have through Christ in the New Testament.

David is not simply trusting in God; he is trusting in the relationship he has with God. Because that's completely God's doing— neither David nor we did anything to earn or merit God's love and grace—we can trust in that relationship.

And then we can move on, just as David did. We can go straight from trusting to rejoicing and praising the Lord.

It's as if David is saying, "I'm going to keep right on trusting you, and because I trust you, now it's time to celebrate with joy and praise."

So once again we see David taking that extra step that doesn't come naturally. Pour out your heart to God, and then listen. Listening and gaining His perspective reminds you that you can trust Him. Then, like David, it's time to celebrate what you have not yet seen, and praise Him.

We could dwell on praising God for an entire devotional, and more. Praise is an indispensable part of prayer, and praise itself can straighten out our perspective. I would even say that sometimes it's good to do nothing in prayer except praise Him.

For now, however, let's get back to mimicking David's approach in his prayer. We've been honest with God. We've listened, and calmed down and trusted Him. Now, celebrate what He is going to do, and celebrate Him. Thank Him, and praise Him.

Praying for self | Praying for believers | Praying with God

Study Guide, Day 5

In Colossians 4:2, Paul wrote, *Continue earnestly in prayer, being vigilant in it with thanksgiving.*

"Continue" has also been translated as "Keep praying" and "Persevere." What do you think is meant by that in connection with prayer?

_____

_____

_____

_____

_____

_____

_____

 "Earnestly" in some translations is rendered as "steadfastly." In others we are told to "devote ourselves to prayer." What do you think Paul means? What's that have to do with prayer?

_____

_____

_____

_____

_____

_____

"Being vigilant" has also been translated as "keeping alert" or "being watchful." What comes to mind when you think about those terms? How does that apply to prayer?

_____

_____

_____

_____

_____

_____

Paul tells us to pray with thanksgiving. He often urges us to pray thankfully, and his frequent expressions of gratitude are a great model. What role does thanksgiving have in prayer?

_____

_____

_____

_____

_____

_____

Praying for self | Praying for believers | Praying with God

Day 6: Because of who He is

Be still, and know that I am God; I will be exalted among the nations, I will be exalted in the earth! Psalm 46:10

You may not realize it, but we have, in effect, completely turned the focus ring.

We've gone from focusing up close and personal on ourselves, to focusing on the infinite—on God. We started out thinking about our circumstances. Focused on ourselves, we let out our feelings to God. And then we left it up to Him. We listened and we trusted, and then we celebrated with thanksgiving and praise.

Maybe you need God's help to get out of an abusive relationship, a difficult position at work, a legal issue or a crushing mountain of debt or other obligations. Maybe you or a family member has a serious health problem. I get it. More importantly, God gets it. Go ahead and ask Him for help each time you feel you need it. Your Father in Heaven cares about you and loves you.

At the same time, we can be blessed even in the most trying times by allowing God to use the circumstances we are in to change us. We need to pray for His perspective and seek His perspective in the Word so we can see what He is teaching us. And we need to pray for His guidance, so we can see where He is leading us.

Then, secure in our knowledge of God and His character, it's time to trust, and to celebrate and praise. To exalt His name.

Praying for self | Praying for believers | Praying with God

Study Guide, Day 6

Here are some verses that give us a picture of God:

For the Lord your God is He who goes with you, to fight for you against your enemies, to save you. Deuteronomy 20:4

God is not a man, that He should lie, nor a son of man, that He should repent. Has He said, and will He not do? Or has He spoken, and will He not make it good? Numbers 23:19

For this is God, our God forever and ever; He will be our guide even to death. Psalm 48:14

My flesh and my heart fail; but God is the strength of my heart and my portion forever. Psalm 73:26

Gracious is the Lord, and righteous; Yes, our God is merciful. Psalm 116:5

Every word of God is pure; He is a shield to those who put their trust in Him. Proverbs 30:5

God is faithful, by whom you were called into the fellowship of His Son, Jesus Christ our Lord. 1 Corinthians 1:9

Which of those descriptions stands out to you? Why?

27

_____

_____

_____

_____

If you were to, like David, write a line of
poetry to describe God, how would it read?

_____

_____

_____

_____

If you were to write a line of poetry about who
God is to you, what would it look like?

_____

_____

_____

_____

If you were to write a line of poetry about
God's work in your life, what would it say?

_____

_____

_____

_____

Praying for self | Praying for believers | Praying with God

Day 7: Getting what we want

Delight yourself also in the Lord, and He shall give you the desires of your heart. Commit your way to the Lord, trust also in Him, and He shall bring it to pass. Psalm 37:4-5

I just gave you what amounts to a formula for prayer:

- Tell God what you're feeling and how you're thinking.
- Listen for His response and His perspective.
- Trust in His love and goodness.
- Praise Him and worship Him.

You want God to answer your prayers, right? And do you want God to give you the answers you want? Well, here's how you do it: Want the things that God wants.

If you find your delight in God, and trust Him, He'll give you what you want because it's what He wants. John wrote something very similar: *Now this is the confidence that we have in Him, that if we ask anything according to His will, He hears us.* (1 John 5:14)

The key is to spend so much quality time with God, in prayer and in His Word, that we think more and more like He thinks.

I headed off to college to become a globe-trotting journalist. But shortly after I began attending a Bible-teaching church, God spoke to me about being a missionary. I did not want to do that.

As the years passed and I grew to know Him and to love Him, I began to see His calling on my life not as a burden, but a promise. I wanted what He wanted for my life. And He made me a missionary. In fact, He made me a globe-trotting journalist for God.

When you allow God to shape your heart—to help you desire what He desires—He can do amazing things in your life. I'm not saying you'll get exactly what you wanted to begin with. But when you find your delight in God, you get what you and He want.

So let's pray. Let's ask God to shape our hearts, and to make His desires our desires. Let's put our future in His hands, and trust Him with it.

Praying for self | Praying for believers | Praying with God

Study Guide, Day 7

Our desires are usually focused on stuff or experiences. We want a new car or a new house. Or we want to visit someplace exotic. I wanted to be a globe-trotting journalist. But I'm only telling you half the story when I say that God gave me the desire of my heart when He made me a missionary.

What God really wants is to be so deeply ingrained in our hearts that He's changing our desires from the inside out. He wants us to be more and more like Him. He's not nearly as concerned whether you're a missionary or a lawyer or a dog groomer, as He is about who you really are. Take a look at Micah 6:6-8:

With what shall I come before the Lord, and bow myself before the High God? Shall I come before Him with burnt offerings, with calves a year old? Will the Lord be pleased with thousands of rams, ten thousand rivers of oil? Shall I give my firstborn for my transgression, the fruit of my body for the sin of my soul?

He has shown you, O man, what is good; and what does the Lord require of you but to do justly, to love mercy, and to walk humbly with your God?

Pleasing God was not—and is not—about offerings or service. It's about who we are, and God sums that up here by urging us to love mercy and walk humbly with Him.

If you ask for that, would God deny you? What kind of changes in your life—changes in who you are and in what you love—do you think you should be asking God for?

_____

_____

_____

_____

_____

_____

_____

Day 8: Shaped and soft

Likewise the Spirit also helps in our weaknesses. For we do not know what we should pray for as we ought, but the Spirit Himself makes intercession for us with groanings which cannot be uttered. Now He who searches the hearts knows what the mind of the Spirit is, because He makes intercession for the saints according to the will of God. Romans 8:26-27

Nothing should keep you from going to God in prayer, even if all you can do is sigh, throw your hands up in dismay, or simply be still. God has this covered—His Spirit is not only interceding for us, but also praying for us according to God's will.

Romans 8 specifically speaks about suffering—about the things we go through because we're children of God in a fallen world. But God also reminds us that nothing can separate us from His love.

The point of the Spirit's prayer is not to remove the suffering, but to use it to grow us and guide us to be more like Christ.

In the midst of the pain and difficulty, it's tough for us to remember that. We might be discouraged, confused or distracted. We might ask for the wrong things or ask with the wrong motivation.

That's why the Spirit is praying for us, "according to the will of God."

As we pray today, let's ask God to stretch our minds a bit, as we start to think about praying not only for ourselves, but for our fellow believers and for what's on God's heart. For now, you don't need to be any more specific than that. You know God wants us to pray for others, and to pray for what He wants. If we're missing something – and let's face it, we often miss things – we can trust the Holy Spirit to address it.

Praying for self | Praying for believers | Praying with God

Study Guide, Day 8

For we do not want you to be ignorant, brethren, of our trouble which came to us in Asia: that we were burdened beyond measure, above strength, so that we despaired even of life. Yes, we had the sentence of death in ourselves, that we should not trust in ourselves but in God who raises the dead, who delivered us from so great a death, and does deliver us; in whom we trust that He will still deliver us, you also helping together in prayer for us, that thanks may be given by many persons on our behalf for the gift granted to us through many. 2 Corinthians 1:8-11

There are probably as many reasons for suffering and hardship as there are believers and circumstances. But I think all of them come down to the point Paul makes here: *that we should not trust in ourselves but in God.*

Has your faith in yourself ever gotten you into trouble? How about your faith in someone else? What should that teach us?

_____

_____

_____

_____

Now think about your faith in God. Trusting Him may have led you into difficulty. But where did that experience lead you in the end?

_____

_____

_____

_____

_____

Note that Paul doesn't dwell on his troubles, but quickly moves to two related topics: the prayers of the Corinthians, and those who will be saved through his work. What does that say to you about how Paul viewed his fellow believers?

_____

_____

_____

_____

_____

Week 2

Praying for your community

Ian Fallis

Day 9: How wide is our focus?

For by one Spirit we were all baptized into one body—whether Jews or Greeks, whether slaves or free—and have all been made to drink into one Spirit. 1 Corinthians 12:13

The whole premise of 1 Corinthians 12—that all believers are one body in Christ—is contrary to our natures.

If you're looking at your class photo, a photo of your family, or any group you are in, who do you look for first? Most people look for themselves. And then they'll judge the overall photo by how they look in the photo.

We are naturally self-focused. In fact, you might even say we're wired to be self-focused. The parietal lobes of our brains keep track of where each of us begins and ends. That's why we don't constantly bump into things. But it also helps isolate us, constantly separating our world between "me" and "everything else."

Yet scientists have discovered that in prayer, that distinction between us and others can melt away. We can embrace the concept that our fellow believers are one with us.

So let's adjust our lens, zooming from a tight telephoto shot of ourselves, to a wide-angle shot of the body of believers. We can and should wrap our heads around the fact that the church is far more than a building where we meet. It's even an understatement to say church is the people who meet there. We are one.

So bow your head and flex your mind. Try to wrap your thoughts around your fellow believers. Then let's pray for others in the body as we have learned to pray for ourselves. Let's focus not on their circumstances, but on the change God desires to bring to their lives.

Study Guide, Day 9

In Colossians 1:9-11, Paul told the church at Colossae how he was praying for them:

For this reason we also, since the day we heard it, do not cease to pray for you, and to ask that you may be filled with the knowledge of His will in all wisdom and spiritual understanding; that you may walk worthy of the Lord, fully pleasing Him, being fruitful in every good work and increasing in the knowledge of God; strengthened with all might, according to His glorious power, for all patience and longsuffering with joy …

What internal changes is Paul asking God to make in the Colossians?

_____

_____

_____

_____

_____

How would that be demonstrated in their actions?

_____

_____

_____

41

People often say they want to know God's will. Is knowing God's will different from being "filled with the knowledge of His will"? How? What does Paul mean by adding, "in all wisdom and spiritual understanding"?

_____

_____

_____

_____

_____

Day 10: Do you want to be effective?

Confess your trespasses to one another, and pray for one another, that you may be healed. The effective, fervent prayer of a righteous man avails much.
James 5:16

The passage in which this verse appears (James 5:13-18) seems to zig and zag through individual and corporate prayer. That may be why so many people take one sentence from verse 16— *"The effective, fervent prayer of a righteous man avails much"* —and interpret it as saying that if we are in right standing with God, praying for His will and praying earnestly, our prayers will be effective.

But there's more to this statement when it's taken in context—and we should always understand any portion of Scripture by what's around it. Before this, James tells us to pray for one another, and after this, gives us an example: Elijah, praying for rain on behalf of all those in Israel who had not bowed to idols.

Therefore, if we adjust our lens and zoom out on this verse, we see that we really should understand the last part of verse 16 to say: When we're in right standing with God, praying for His will and praying earnestly for our fellow believers, our prayers will be effective.

So let's pray for God to give us His perspective on our own lives, so we can see where we are or are not lining up with His will for us. Let's pray for His will to be done in the lives of our fellow believers, and pray for them.

Praying for self | Praying for believers | Praying with God

Study Guide, Day 10

In Ephesians 1:17-19, Paul writes that he prayed *that the God of our Lord Jesus Christ, the Father of glory, may give to you the spirit of wisdom and revelation in the knowledge of Him, the eyes of your understanding being enlightened; that you may know what is the hope of His calling, what are the riches of the glory of His inheritance in the saints, and what is the exceeding greatness of His power toward us who believe ...*

In your own words, take note of each of the things Paul is asking God to give the church at Ephesus.

_____

_____

_____

_____

_____

_____

_____

_____

_____

Now go back through those, putting an "H" by those that have to do with Heaven and a "W" by those that have to do with the World. What do you see?

_____

_____

_____

_____

_____

If God grants Paul's prayer, whose perspective will the Ephesians have? What changes will that kind of perspective make in their lives?

_____

_____

_____

_____

_____

Day 11: Getting on the same page

There is one body and one Spirit, just as you were called in one hope of your calling; one Lord, one faith, one baptism; one God and Father of all, who is above all, and through all, and in you all.
Ephesians 4:4-6

English doesn't differentiate between you (singular) and you (plural). So the translators of this passage resorted to the Southern vernacular to make this passage abundantly clear: Be united, because God the Father is in y'all.

How many bodies are we? Our brains tell us each of us is a body. But Paul tells us that together we're one body, just as there is one Spirit.

Paul even tells us how we can be united, and it starts with walking the walk we were called to walk: Humble, patient, loving and peace-seeking.

That's important, because if there's one body, that means that your church and my church and—oh my—*that* church over *there* too—are one. You know which church I'm talking about.

- The one that emphasizes the wrong things (because our church has it right).
- The one that has those people who irritate us and are unteachable (because we're never irritating and always teachable).
- The one that isn't loving (because we always are).
- The one that created the division in the first place (because they, not us, were at fault).

Wait a minute. What happened to being humble, patient, loving and peace-seeking?

We are one. *Pray for one another* means to pray for them too. And I don't think God means, "pray for them to change so they're just like us." I think He wants you and me to pray that all of us, through humility, patience, love and peace-seeking, work together for His glory in unison.

Will you pray for that right now?

Study Guide, Day 11

Unity of the believers was important to Paul, and it's important to God. He exhorted the Philippians to have the mind of Christ: humble and united. And he told the Thessalonians (1 Thessalonians 3:12-13) he was praying for their unity in love:

And may the Lord make you increase and abound in love to one another and to all, just as we do to you, so that He may establish your hearts blameless in holiness before our God and Father at the coming of our Lord Jesus Christ with all His saints.

Why do you think God makes such a big deal about the unity of believers?

_____

_____

_____

_____

_____

How is love important to unity?

_____

_____

_____

_____

What's the role of humility in unity?

_____

_____

_____

_____

_____

Paul told the Thessalonians he wanted them to abound in love to one *another "so that He may establish your hearts blameless … before God."* What's that imply about the condition of our relationship with God if we're not united?

_____

_____

_____

_____

_____

Day 12: Diversity in the body

But to each one of us grace was given according to the measure of Christ's gift. Therefore He says: "When He ascended on high, He … gave gifts to men." Ephesians 4:7-8

Immediately after talking about y'all, Paul begins to talk about each of us. He writes in verses 11-16 about some of the gifts, as he does in 1 Corinthians 12:1-12. And in the following verses he ties it all together. We're all one, but we're each uniquely gifted for a specific purpose, none more important or less important than another: *But now indeed there are many members, yet one body. And the eye cannot say to the hand, "I have no need of you"; nor again the head to the feet, "I have no need of you."* (1 Corinthians 12:20-21)

Paul's examples are intended to be absurd. Your eye can see a coffee cup, but it can't pick it up without your hand. Your head can't get anywhere without your feet. For that matter, the only one that can talk is your head, and only with the help of your mouth.

I am recovering from a leg injury. I could not sit for long, stand for long or walk for long.

When I did walk, I called on other muscles to work harder so the damaged one didn't have to do as much. That strained those muscles. I finally found that stretching and walking normally allowed my whole leg to heal.

Do you know what we need to stretch? We need to stretch our minds around these facts:

- Believers are different … and God loves them all unconditionally.
- Believers have different gifts … and no one is better or more valuable than another.
- Believers have different roles … and sometimes we need to step out of the way so others can fulfill their roles.

Only in prayer will we find the discernment to embody these principles. Only in prayer will we find the ability to value others as God values them. Prayer strengthens the community by freeing us each to fill the roles we are given.

Let's pray for discernment. Pray that God helps us love people who are different, and value them as He does. Pray that we each take on the roles we're intended to, and that we get out of the way and let others do His work.

Study Guide, Day 12

Read beyond today's passage in Ephesians 4, and in verses 11-13 you come to this:

And He Himself gave some to be apostles, some prophets, some evangelists, and some pastors and teachers, for the equipping of the saints ... till we all come to the unity of the faith ...

And then in verse 16, this: *"... the whole body, joined and knit together by what every joint supplies, according to the effective working by which every part does its share, causes growth of the body for the edifying of itself in love."*

When we all do our part, what does Paul say happens?

_____

_____

_____

_____

_____

What can you think of that you or other believers do that prevent people from effectively working together to build up the body of believers?

_____

_____

_____

_____

_____

What can we do in order to help others take on their roles?

_____

_____

_____

_____

_____

Day 13: Discover and fulfill your role

But the manifestation of the Spirit is given to each one for the profit of all. 1 Corinthians 12:7

Remember what you have and why. We have spiritual gifts *"for the equipping of the saints for the work of ministry, for the edifying of the body of Christ"* (Ephesians 4:12). And Paul writes in the next verse that this leads to *"the unity of the faith."*

Paul wraps up his discussion of the body of Christ in Ephesians 4:16 with this: *"The whole body, joined and knit together by what every joint supplies, according to the effective working by which every part does its share, causes growth of the body for the edifying of itself in love."*

Do you know what your spiritual gift is? All believers have one. If you don't know what it is, ask God to reveal it to you through your pastor or other teachers or leaders in your church. Seek the Lord and those qualified for help discovering it. You can find tools online for this, but I recommend you go to your local body of believers. That's where, in most cases, you'll be expected to use your gift.

If you know what your gift is, are you using it to build up the body? That's what it's for. It's not vain to ask for opportunities to use your gift. But you shouldn't assume you know exactly what those opportunities are. Again, go to your church leaders. Ask them in a spirit of humility where your gift can be used.

And pray for opportunities to use your spiritual gift, to build up the body and foster unity. Even if you've known what your gift is for years, and you've been using it, perhaps there are other ways God wants you to use it. Perhaps you can do more to encourage unity.

Praying for self | Praying for believers | Praying with God

Study Guide, Day 13:

The verse we looked at today—1 Corinthians 12:7—is only the preamble to an important passage:

But the manifestation of the Spirit is given to each one for the profit of all: for to one is given the word of wisdom through the Spirit, to another the word of knowledge through the same Spirit ... But one and the same Spirit works all these things, distributing to each one individually as He wills.

Who gave you a spiritual gift? And why?

_____

_____

_____

_____

_____

What are the results of you using your spiritual gift?

_____

_____

_____

_____

_____

If those are the results of using your gift, what do you think happens if you don't use it?

_____

_____

_____

_____

_____

What do you need to ask God to do, in order for you to use your gift effectively?

_____

_____

_____

_____

_____

Day 14: Love in action

Now the multitude of those who believed were of one heart and one soul; neither did anyone say that any of the things he possessed was his own, but they had all things in common. Acts 4:32

It's odd to me that giving to our fellow believers is so rare today. It's one of the only types of giving spoken about in the New Testament. We see this not only in Acts, but in several of the epistles, where Paul talks about an offering for the suffering believers in Jerusalem.

In fact, in 2 Corinthians 8, Paul says the poverty-stricken believers in Macedonia—having first given themselves to God (verse 5)—freely gave more than they could afford, even begging him for the opportunity to be part of the effort. He urged the wealthy Corinthians to also give, so that "your abundance may supply their lack" (verse 14).

We foster unity when we demonstrate love for one another and for God through generosity to our fellow believers.

I'm not going to ask you to pray about whether you ought to give. You already know you should. The Bible says so. I'm not going to ask you to pray about how much you can afford. The Bible encourages us to follow God's leading and act in faith—perhaps even giving more than we can afford, and trusting God to take care of us.

Instead, I'm asking you to pray for wisdom and discernment to see opportunities to foster unity by giving to your fellow believers, and for the courage and faith to act on those opportunities.

Praying for self | Praying for believers | Praying with God

Study Guide, Day 14

Paul told the Corinthians that the Macedonians gave generously after *"they first gave themselves to the Lord"* (2 Corinthians 8:5). What do you suppose that means?

_____

_____

_____

_____

Paul also wrote about giving in a letter to one of the churches in Macedonia, at Philippi. After telling the Philippians how much he valued them, told them in Philippians 1:9-11 how he prayed for them:

And this I pray, that your love may abound still more and more in knowledge and all discernment, that you may approve the things that are excellent, that you may be sincere and without offense till the day of Christ, being filled with the fruits of righteousness which are by Jesus Christ, to the glory and praise of God.

The book of Philippians is Paul's response to the church's expression of love through a generous gift to his ministry. Over and over again in Philippians, Paul comes back to the topic of love. It makes sense. Generosity is one of the primary ways we show love—generosity with our resources, our time, our patience, and more. And none of those are actually ours. If we're children of God, they're His. How are you being generous?

_____

_____

_____

_____

What are some other ways you could be more generous?

_____

_____

_____

_____

What would God have to do in your heart to make you more generous?

_____

_____

_____

_____

_____

Will you ask Him to do that?

Day 15: Loving believers is practice for loving the lost

If someone says, "I love God," and hates his brother, he is a liar; for he who does not love his brother whom he has seen, how can he love God whom he has not seen? 1 John 4:20

Sometimes it's not easy to love our brothers and sisters.

Our brothers and sisters can gossip. On occasion they undermine each other. They may compete for things like power and funding and prestige and popularity. They can be greedy and self-serving.

They sound like people, don't they? People Christ died for. People in whom God still has work to do.

People like you and me.

John effectively writes that we can't say we love God if we don't love our fellow believers. And if we can't love our fellow believers, what chance do we have of loving the world?

Well, none.

The answer isn't to try harder. The answer is to pray, and let God love others through us.

Face it: People are unlovely, and will be unlovely, and sometimes increasingly so. That can lead us to become cynical or bitter or uncaring—which are quite contrary to being loving. Pray for God to enable and empower you to love.

And when we love our brothers and sisters, and act on that love, we're better prepared to step forward in unity to address the need that's on God's heart.

THE FOCUS OF PRAYER

Praying for self | Praying for believers | Praying with God

Study Guide, Day 15

It's interesting that after Paul tells the Colossians and Ephesians how he is praying for them, he has a similar request for each church:

… Praying also for us, that God would open to us a door for the word, to speak the mystery of Christ, for which I am also in chains, that I may make it manifest, as I ought to speak. Colossians 4:3-4

… For me, that utterance may be given to me, that I may open my mouth boldly to make known the mystery of the gospel, for which I am an ambassador in chains; that in it I may speak boldly, as I ought to speak. Ephesians 6:19-20

What, in your own words, is Paul asking them to pray for him?

_____

_____

_____

_____

_____

_____

Are you and your fellow believers also ambassadors? What part of this prayer would apply to you?

_____

_____

_____

_____

_____

How is sharing the gospel an expression of love?

_____

_____

_____

_____

_____

Week 3

Praying for what's on God's heart

Ian Fallis

Day 16: How moving are our prayers?

Then He said to them, "The harvest truly is great, but the laborers are few; therefore pray the Lord of the harvest to send out laborers into His harvest." Luke 10:2

Imagine this: You walk into a prayer meeting and sit down next to a friend. You're chatting away about how your day has been, when you realize a hush has fallen over the people behind you. And then you see why. Jesus Himself walks down the aisle past you and sits in the front row. Of course He'd sit in the front row, right?

I don't know about you, but I'd get out my phone and snap a picture of that.

And what if He raised His hand to share a prayer request? Well, I'd switch to video. I'd want pictures that moved, and sound. Then I'd post that video to Facebook and YouTube and, if He kept it brief, to Vine. I'd want the whole world to hear Jesus' prayer request. Wouldn't you?

And what if, a few weeks later, He showed up somewhere else with the same request? Can you imagine the impact it would have on

God's people if Jesus shared a prayer request, and it was important enough for Him to share it twice?

Well, He did just that. Not here and now. But then and there. Luke 10:2 and Matthew 9:37-38 contain almost identical prayer requests from Jesus, shared on two different occasions. In Luke 10, He shares this as He commissions the seventy-two to spread the word that the Kingdom of God is at hand. In Matthew 9, we're told that Jesus was moved with compassion for the needs He saw, and said, *"The harvest truly is plentiful, but the laborers are few. Therefore pray the Lord of the harvest to send out laborers into His harvest."*

This request was so important that Jesus is recorded as sharing it twice. Do you think He meant for us to take notice? I do. I think integrating Jesus' prayer request is vital to balancing our prayer lives.

So let's keep it simple and straightforward today. Pray to the Lord of the harvest to send out laborers into His harvest.

Study Guide, Day 16

When people talk about Jesus and prayer, they often refer to the Lord's Prayer, in Luke 11:2-4 and Matthew 6:9-13. Look those up. What does Jesus tell us to pray about?

_____

_____

_____

_____

Some also bring up John 17, when Jesus prayed before going to the Garden of Gethsemane. What does Jesus pray for His disciples? (John 17:6-19)

_____

_____

_____

_____

What does He pray for believers? (John 17:20-26)

_____

_____

_____

_____

The Lord's Prayer is the answer to what question in Luke 11:1? Now look at Matthew 6:9. Is Jesus giving prayer requests, or is He talking about how they should pray?

_____

_____

_____

_____

What were the circumstances of Jesus' prayer before going to the Garden? Are there any prayer requests?

_____

_____

_____

_____

If Luke 10:2 and Matthew 9:37-38 are not only the same prayer request stated twice, but Jesus' only prayer request, how important should this request be to us? Do you need to re-order priorities?

_____

_____

_____

_____

_____

Praying for self | Praying for believers | Praying with God

Day 17: The desire of God

*Then He said to them, "The harvest truly is great, but the laborers are few; therefore **pray** the Lord of the harvest to send out laborers into His harvest."*
Luke 10:2

I'm sure you've asked people to pray for you. You've probably also asked people to pray for family members and friends. And we expect people to pray for us and our friends. But do you expect them to make those prayers personal? To take them on as if they were their own desires?

That's what Jesus is asking us to do.

Where the Bible says, *"pray the Lord of the harvest,"* the word Jesus is quoted as using for "pray" is *deomai*. The words "pray" or "beseech" appear seventy-nine times in the King James Version, but only thirteen times is the Greek word *deomai*.

It actually means "to desire."

Jesus did not simply say this is a good thing to pray about. He didn't just say this was important to Him. He's asking us to make this important to us, and to pray earnestly for this.

73

Jesus wants us to make this prayer, our prayer. It's on His heart. He wants it to be on our hearts. I think it would be appropriate to get down on our knees and plead with God for laborers. It's His desire; it should be ours as well.

Study Guide, Day 17

Do you remember the best way to get what you want? Want what God wants. *Delight yourself also in the Lord, and He shall give you the desires of your heart.* (Psalm 37:4) Now we see Jesus asking us, twice, to "desire" for God to send laborers to His harvest.

God wants us to make His desires, our desires, and He specifically asks us to embody this one. How are you doing with that? Write down how you would characterize your heart attitudes toward the Great Commission—to make disciples of all nations.

_____

_____

_____

_____

_____

This study will help you; I encourage you to keep going. But let's make it personal.

What changes can you make today to your prayer life that will help you make God's desire to reach all nations, your desire?

_____

_____

_____

_____

_____

What changes can you make today in your
Bible reading, study and memorization that
will help you make God's desire to reach all
nations, your desire?

_____

_____

_____

_____

What changes can you make today in the way
you prioritize your use of resources — time,
money, possessions and relationships — that
will help you make God's desire to reach all
nations, your desire?

_____

_____

_____

_____

Praying for self | Praying for believers | Praying with God

Day 18: Too few laborers

Then He said to them, "The harvest truly is great, but the laborers are few; therefore pray the Lord of the harvest **to send out laborers** *into His harvest."* Luke 10:2

This is not a time to get bogged down with details.

I've heard at least a dozen different estimates of how many people groups are still unreached, based on a dozen different methods and systems. And I'm sure if we put a dozen believers in a room, we'd hear a dozen different definitions of what a laborer is. Neither of those is terribly important compared to a few overarching facts:

- The harvest is not yet complete.
- There's still a lot of work to do.
- God has given this work to His people.

And the fact is, the numbers all agree that thousands of people groups with millions and millions of people are still unreached.

Let's think people themselves. Men, women and children are living and dying with no access to the abundant, eternal life that Jesus died to make available to all of us.

It's not unusual for people groups who hear a clear presentation of the gospel for the first time to wail for their relatives who died without access to the Truth. Or to ask, "How long have you known this? Why did it take so long for you to bring this to us?"

God could—and can—use supernatural means to draw people to Himself. He also uses technology, such as radio broadcasts, MP3 recordings of lessons and Scripture, and websites.

But the non-negotiable fact is that it takes a disciple to make a disciple. To carry out the work of His harvest takes people.

Pray for laborers. More are still needed.

Praying for self | Praying for believers | Praying with God

Study Guide, Day 18

As early as the First Century, local concerns pushed "the nations" out of the picture. Diotrephes (3 John 9-11) not only wanted nothing to do with missionaries, he didn't want anyone else helping them. But in 3 John 5-8, John commends Gaius for his help:

Beloved, you do faithfully whatever you do for the brethren and for strangers, who have borne witness of your love before the church. If you send them forward on their journey in a manner worthy of God, you will do well, because they went forth for His name's sake, taking nothing from the Gentiles. We therefore ought to receive such, that we may become fellow workers for the truth.

We know from the context that John is writing about missionaries. John writes in 3 John 5, *"whatever you do for the brethren."* What kinds of things could fall into "whatever" you could do to help missionaries today?

_____

_____

_____

_____

In 3 John 6, John refers to *"send[ing] them forward in a manner worthy of God."* In the First Century, missionaries traveled from church to church, leaving each one with more of what they needed to reach their ministry destination. What can you specifically do to help missionaries with their next step? (Hint: If you don't know, ask a missionary. If you don't know one, find one.)

_____

_____

_____

_____

_____

John tells us in 3 John 8 that *"we ... ought to receive such,"* or in some translations, *"support such men."* What can you do to show hospitality to missionaries, or to help them financially?

_____

_____

_____

_____

_____

Day 19: Harvesting is hard work

*Then He said to them, "**The harvest truly is great**, but the laborers are few; therefore pray the Lord of the harvest to send out laborers into His harvest."* Luke 10:2

I loved having a vegetable garden. It was wonderful to step outside and harvest a couple of ripe tomatoes for a salad. But that's not really the kind of harvest Jesus is talking about here.

He's not talking about a small garden plot in a yard in the suburbs. He's talking about an expanse of land, tilled, planted, watered and weeded in order to reach the day of harvest. Jesus wasn't using a gardening analogy; He was using a farming analogy.

Any farmer will agree that the harvest is a great thing. It's the day all that hard work pays off. But it's also a far cry from plucking a couple of tomatoes and stepping inside to make a salad. It's hard work in and of itself.

And it's not something you can put off.

For a home gardener, it's a bummer if you let a tomato drop off the vine and rot because you didn't pluck it at the right time. It's a catastrophe for the farmer if thousands of tomatoes fall and are lost forever.

Jesus is not saying, "Hey, look, it's all just waiting for workers. It's easy!" He's saying, "There's a big job out there, and it needs to be done, and it needs to be done now."

This should drive us to pray with urgency and passion for laborers. Let's do that.

Study Guide, Day 19

Mourning for the people of Israel, lost in their idolatry, Jeremiah wrote: *The harvest is past, the summer is ended, and we are not saved.* (Jeremiah 8:20) His people were rebellious, yet God cared about them. What do you see about God's character in this?

_____

_____

_____

_____

_____

Likewise, Paul wrote: *The Lord is not slack concerning His promise, as some count slackness, but is longsuffering toward us, not willing that any should perish, but that all should come to repentance.* (2 Peter 3:9) What's this say to you about God?

_____

_____

_____

_____

_____

_____

In 2 Peter 3:10, Peter tells us the day of the Lord is coming, when *"both the earth and the works that are in it will be burned up."* What's this say about the time we have for the harvest?

_____

_____

_____

_____

_____

Look back at 2 Peter 3:9. Who does Peter say God is patient toward? Why?

_____

_____

_____

_____

_____

What are you going to do different today so that your life better reflects God's desire that people have an opportunity to know Him?

_____

_____

_____

_____

_____

Praying for self | Praying for believers | Praying with God

Day 20: Sending is vital

*Then He said to them, "The harvest truly is great, but the laborers are few; therefore pray the Lord of the harvest **to send out laborers** into His harvest."* Luke 10:2

It's not just that harvesting is hard work. The work that's left to do is often in the world's hard places.

- Geography makes people hard to get to.
- Countries can make it difficult for a Christian to enter.
- Cultures can create hard soil, where it's just plain tough to get seeds to sprout.

In some places, all three are true. That's why Jesus tells us to ask God to send these laborers out. Without a clear sense that God is in charge and directing their steps, these laborers cannot last.

But that's not the only thing the Bible says about sending.

After telling us that *"whoever calls on the name of the Lord shall be saved"* in Romans 10:13, Paul makes the point that someone needs to come and share God's truth, and in verse 15 writes, *"And how shall they preach unless they are sent?"*

Paul and his companions were sent out by God, and by the church at Antioch. (Acts 13:1-3) This harvest is the task before all believers, and praying is one part of the picture.

You may have heard "pray, give or go." But it's more correct to say, "pray, send and go." Every believer is called to pray for laborers. Since this task belongs to all of us, we need to share the responsibility by sending— by giving not simply to contribute, but giving in order to equip people for ministry. That means giving not what we feel like giving, but giving generously and sacrificially in order for laborers to serve. And we can all "go" wherever we are.

Do you know a missionary? Pray for them daily, and pray specifically whether God wants you to help send them. If you don't know a missionary, find one—preferably one with a connection to your church. Pray for them, and pray about being part of their sending team. Pray also for God to direct you to the place He wants you to go.

Praying for self | Praying for believers | Praying with God

Study Guide, Day 20

A couple of days ago we looked at 3 John. What do you suppose John meant when he wrote, *Therefore we ought to support such men, so that we may be fellow workers with the truth* (3 John 8, NASB)?

_____

_____

_____

_____

_____

When Jesus sent out the seventy to proclaim the Kingdom (Luke 10), he told them, *"the laborer is worthy of his wages"* (Luke 10:7). When He sent out the twelve disciples, He said, *"the worker is worthy of his support"* (Matthew 10:10, NASB). What does that say to you about what missionaries receive?

_____

_____

_____

_____

_____

In 1 Corinthians 9:4-14, Paul argues that no missionary should go *"at his own expense"* (1 Corinthians 9:7), and *"the Lord directed those who proclaim the gospel to get their living from the gospel"* (1 Corinthians 9:14, NASB). What do you think Paul is saying about missionary support?

_____

_____

_____

_____

_____

How would you apply these passages to your own use of the resources that God has provided for your needs and for His work?

_____

_____

_____

_____

_____

Day 21: It's not an isolated prayer

Go therefore and make disciples of all the nations …
Matthew 28:19

If Jesus simply asked us, twice, to *"pray the Lord of the harvest to send out laborers into His harvest,"* that would be important. But that's not the only thing the Bible says on this topic.

It's a central theme of Scripture, beginning with God's covenant with Abram in Genesis 12: *"In you all the families of the earth shall be blessed."*

God repeated the theme in Isaiah 49:6: *"I will also give You as a light to the Gentiles, that You should be My salvation to the ends of the earth."*

When the Great Commission is shared, it is not one verse in one Gospel. It is found in different forms, at different times, across all four Gospels and in Acts.

And we see the theme come to fruition in Revelation 5:9, when the twenty-four elders sing, *"You are worthy to take the scroll, and to open its seals; for You were slain, and have redeemed us to God by Your blood out of every tribe and tongue and people and nation."*

It really should be as simple as remembering John 3:16. God loves you. He loves me. He loves all the people of the world. And it's for all the people of the world that He gave His Son.

Remember that we looked at the fact that when our prayers line up with the will of God, we'll see answers? Praying for laborers so the world can hear sounds an awful lot like the will of God, and therefore an indispensable part of a balanced prayer life.

Pray now that you and other believers make the most of opportunities to share Christ with lost people living near you, and that God sends believers to those who have no witness near them. Pray that their hearts will be open to the truth, and they will find salvation in Christ.

Praying for self | Praying for believers | Praying with God

Study Guide, Day 21

The Great Commandment (Matthew 22:36-40) is as important as the Great Commission:

"Teacher, which is the great commandment in the law?"

Jesus said to him, "'You shall love the LORD your God with all your heart, with all your soul, and with all your mind.' This is the first and great commandment. And the second is like it: 'You shall love your neighbor as yourself.' On these two commandments hang all the Law and the Prophets."

How do the Great Commission and the Great Commandment fit together? How is *"make disciples of all the nations"* (Matthew 28:19) an expression of God's love, and how does joining in it express your love for God?

_____

_____

_____

_____

_____

_____

Who is my neighbor? In a passage very similar to the Great Commandment, Jesus answers that question. Read Luke 10:26-37. How would you summarize Jesus' definition of "neighbor"?

_____

_____

_____

_____

_____

What parallels do you see between Jesus' definition of "neighbor" and all nations?

_____

_____

_____

_____

_____

_____

Day 22: Trusting His promises

After this I looked, and there before me was a great multitude that no one could count, from every nation, tribe, people and language, standing before the throne and before the Lamb. They were wearing white robes and were holding palm branches in their hands. Revelation 7:9

It's easy to lose track of the most important things in our busy modern world. We fixate on the here and now. Our daily struggles and triumphs fill our minds.

And now I've gone and complicated it all, urging you to rethink the way you pray for yourself, and to pray for your fellow believers and pray the prayer that's on God's heart.

So before we talk about how we balance all that, let me simplify things. Let's look at what God has promised us.

You will be conformed to the image of Christ, growing and maturing. That's not a burden on you; it's a promise from God. You and I are utterly and completely unable to conform ourselves to the image of Christ. While we must act—while we must choose to do those things that keep us aligned with His

93

will for us—we're dependent on Him, so we ought to trust Him.

Believers will be unified and, in that, God will be glorified. Again, this is a promise. You and I and other believers cannot be truly unified apart from the work of God in us and through us. Trust in Him and in this promise as well.

Fulfilling the Great Commission is also the Lord's work. It's still a huge task, and it's going to be accomplished through millions of partnerships that are, in proportion to the task, microscopic. Only He can weave those together, and since we know there will be a multitude around the throne from every nation, tribe, people and language, we can see that as a promise as well.

Take time to think on God as we will one day see Him. Allow His presence to fill you with awe and reverence. Praise Him and worship Him. Petition Him for the love and strength and courage you need to be the ambassador of Jesus in your world.

Praying for self | Praying for believers | Praying with God

Study Guide, Day 22

Paul wrote to the Philippians, *I thank my God upon every remembrance of you … being confident of this very thing, that He who has begun a good work in you will complete it until the day of Jesus Christ.* (Philippians 1:3, 6) What does this promise mean to you?

_____

_____

_____

_____

_____

In Jeremiah, God said, *For I know the thoughts that I think toward you, says the LORD, thoughts of peace and not of evil, to give you a future and a hope.* (Jeremiah 29:11) Do God's plans not only include you, but have your good in mind? What's that mean to you?

_____

_____

_____

_____

_____

Isaiah wrote, *He gives power to the weak, and to those who have no might He increases strength. Even the youths shall faint and be weary, and the young men shall utterly fall, but those who wait on the LORD shall renew their strength; they shall mount up with wings like eagles, they shall run and not be weary, they shall walk and not faint.* (Isaiah 40:29-31) What hope can you have in God?

_____

_____

_____

_____

God's plans not only include you, but include your good. He will continue to work in you, and to give you strength. So what can you trust Him for today? For what do you want Him to give you faith and courage?

_____

_____

_____

_____

_____

Will you ask Him for those things, and let Him continue to change you?

Week 4

Bringing it all into focus

Ian Fallis

Day 23: How can this be possible?

But seek first the kingdom of God and His righteousness, and all these things shall be added to you. Matthew 6:33

Have you ever grabbed your camera to take a photo at just the right time, only to be disappointed because it was out of focus, or focused on the wrong place? Wouldn't it be great if you could take the picture, then focus later?

Actually, you can. There's a novel camera technology called "light field photography" that allows people to choose the point of focus—or even bring the whole photo into focus—as they look at the photo later.

I have a hard time wrapping my head around that. It seems like magic. It's not supernatural, of course. It's technology. Technology is giving us powers and abilities that people used to just dream about.

That's sort of what we're going to do next. We're going to explore how these three seemingly unrelated topics—praying properly for ourselves, praying for our fellow believers, and praying the prayer on God's heart — can unify in a focused prayer life.

We're going to start reordering our prayers. We're going to put God first, then others, and then ourselves. Why does God come first?

- He's God. He should come first.
- What's on God's heart is clear and specific, while we often don't know how to pray for others or even ourselves.
- Putting God first helps put our priorities in order, and orders our prayers.

Focusing on God first is the best way to bring everything else into focus. So let's get to work. Start by reading a Psalm of praise. Here are some choices: Psalm 18, 21, 28, 30, 32, 34, 36, 40, 41, 66, 105, 106, 111, 113, 116, 117, 135, 136, 138, 146, and 147. And yes, you can read more than one, you overachiever.

Then simply pray for what's on God's heart. Ask Him to send laborers into His harvest. Pause to listen. How long is between you and God. Then pray for your fellow believers. Pause for Him again. And then pray for yourself. And listen.

Praying with God | Praying for believers | Praying for self

Study Guide, Day 23

"Therefore do not worry, saying, 'What shall we eat?' or 'What shall we drink?' or 'What shall we wear?' For after all these things the Gentiles seek. For your heavenly Father knows that you need all these things. But seek first the kingdom of God and His righteousness, and all these things shall be added to you. Therefore do not worry about tomorrow, for tomorrow will worry about its own things. Sufficient for the day is its own trouble." (Matthew 6:31-34)

When we jump into prayer "me-first," we tend to focus on things we identify as our needs. We talk to God about food, clothing, housing, and other material things, and about the jobs and money to get them. But Jesus, in the Sermon on the Mount, said that's backwards. He said God already knows we need these things, and we ought to focus first on seeking God.

And you have to love the fact that Jesus really, truly understands us. How else could He talk about worry and trouble so clearly?

What does it mean to you to *"seek first the kingdom of God and His righteousness"*?

_____

_____

_____

_____

Is there one thing you've been praying about or worrying about that you think you should put aside? What is it, and why should you stop?

_____

_____

_____

_____

_____

What are you going to do differently in your prayer life to seek God first?

_____

_____

_____

_____

_____

_____

Day 24: Putting God first

Jesus said to him, "You shall love the Lord your God with all your heart, with all your soul, and with all your mind." Matthew 22:37

Putting God first is about more than order. It's also about priority and perspective.

We know we should want what God wants. But we get distracted by shiny things, pretty stuff, awesome gadgets and cool gear. Or by excitement, or fun. Travel and leisure. Games.

There's often room in our lives for things like that when we're walking with God. But those things are never supposed to be the focus of our lives. We need to step back daily and remember that Jesus left us with a prayer request that was clearly important to Him. That has to be a great definition of what God wants:

"The harvest truly is great, but the laborers are few; therefore pray the Lord of the harvest to send out laborers into His harvest." (Luke 10:2)

Today, a laborer carefully chooses the words in an unfamiliar language to build a relationship with her neighbor—a relationship she hopes will someday give her an opportunity to share the gospel. Will you pray for her?

Another laborer struggles to keep up with the other men on the jungle trail, anxious to invest time in understanding not only the way they speak, but the way they think, so he can present the Truth clearly. Will you pray for him?

Somewhere else, a laborer kneels by the bedside of a dying woman, agonizing as he tries to wrap concrete words around abstract concepts so she has an opportunity to meet Jesus. Will you pray?

Daily, His laborers need His sending power to renew and refresh them for the work ahead. So each day, please remember that. Don't just pray for these laborers. Let their situations and challenges pierce your heart and make Jesus' prayer, your prayer.

Ask God to send them forward. Make that a priority. Work to see the world in light of the importance Christ placed on this prayer.

Study Guide, Day 24

I think the believers at Philippi, in Macedonia, got it. Read what Paul said about them when he was writing to the wealthy Corinthians about helping believers in Jerusalem:

Moreover, brethren, we make known to you the grace of God bestowed on the churches of Macedonia: that in a great trial of affliction the abundance of their joy and their deep poverty abounded in the riches of their liberality. For I bear witness that according to their ability, yes, and beyond their ability, they were freely willing, imploring us with much urgency that we would receive the gift and the fellowship of the ministering to the saints. And not only as we had hoped, but they first gave themselves to the Lord, and then to us by the will of God. (2 Corinthians 8:1-5)

Paul characterized the Philippians as rich and poor. How were they poor? How were they rich? Which is better?

_____

_____

_____

_____

They gave more than they were able to—another translation says, *"more than they could afford."* They "implored" Paul to let them help. How would you characterize their attitude toward giving?

_____

_____

_____

_____

But here's why I say they got it: All this stems from the fact that *"they first gave themselves to the Lord."* What's that mean to you?

_____

_____

_____

_____

_____

What do you need to do, in order to give yourself to the Lord?

_____

_____

_____

_____

_____

Day 25: Praying for the senders

I thank my God upon every remembrance of you, always in every prayer of mine making request for you all with joy, for your fellowship in the gospel from the first day until now. Philippians 1:3-5

Paul frequently writes that he thanks God for his fellow believers. He specifically thanks God for the Philippians' "fellowship in the gospel"—their participation in his ministry as a missionary, in giving, encouragement and prayer.

If we're going to follow biblical examples—and that's a good thing—we ought to start with an attitude of gratitude toward our fellow believers.

Keeping in mind what Jesus asked us to pray about, we should be thankful that men and women are coming forward to serve, and pray that God works in more hearts so more go out.

We should be thankful for the men and women who are sending those people, and pray for more senders. And we should be thankful for those standing with them in prayer, and ask God for more people to pray daily.

Let's do that, right now. But be specific. Pray for individuals you know who fall into those groups. Pray for people who go, people who send and people who pray, as well as people who are considering going, sending or praying.

Praying with God | Praying for believers | Praying for self

Study Guide, Day 25

Thankfulness in prayer is like praise in prayer: it's easily the subject of an entire devotional in and of itself. For our purposes, let's look at these two verses:

In everything give thanks; for this is the will of God in Christ Jesus for you. (I Thessalonians 5:18)

Giving thanks always for all things to God the Father in the name of our Lord Jesus Christ. (Ephesians 5:20)

We often give thanks for the good things in our lives. Which things or circumstances or relationships are we told to give thanks for?

_____

_____

_____

_____

_____

Some people would say they are thankful, even though they don't express it. Others say thanks, but do not seem to live in a way that a grateful person would. Is there anything about these verses that says giving thanks and being thankful go hand in hand?

_____

_____

_____

_____

_____

Yesterday we saw that when the Philippians heard about the needs of the believers in Jerusalem, they began *imploring us with much urgency that we would receive the gift.* Does it sound as if they were grateful for the opportunity to give? Why?

_____

_____

_____

_____

_____

Are you grateful? Do you respond like the Philippians to opportunities to give? Are you honored, or are you grudging, when someone asks you for help? Does response reveal a heart problem or a healthy attitude?

_____

_____

_____

_____

Day 26: Praying for the laborers

Continue earnestly in prayer ... praying also for us, that God would open to us a door for the word, to speak the mystery of Christ, for which I am also in chains. Colossians 4:2-3

It just makes sense that if Jesus asked us to pray for God to send laborers, we should also be praying for the laborers themselves. Paul certainly asked people to pray for him.

Let's start with three areas of prayer to keep in mind for missionaries, based on how Jesus and Paul asked us to pray:

- Pray that they have a clear sense that God is sending them. Pray that daily God gives them encouragement, strength and provision for their work.
- Pray for opportunities for them to share the gospel and make disciples.
- Pray for safety, and for perseverance, wisdom and boldness in the face of persecution, hardship and opposition.

Are you praying daily for a specific laborer? Are your prayers specific—are you digging through their newsletters for prayer requests? Have you asked them how you can pray for them? If you contacted a missionary and told them you wanted to pray for them daily, that would also encourage them.

If you're not already praying for a specific individual, couple or family, now is a good time to start. Here are three ways to find one:

- Choose a laborer your church is already involved with. Ask your pastor or other church leader for help contacting them.
- Subscribe to NTM's weekly prayer update, and connect with an individual, couple or family mentioned there. (**usa.ntm.org/subscribe-to-email-updates**)
- Contact a missions organization and ask if any missionaries are living in your area—based there or on home assignment—with whom you can meet and get involved.

Don't agonize over the organization or the specific person or the type or place of service. It's not like you're going to pray for someone daily, then get to Heaven and hear God say, "I didn't want anyone praying for that missionary." So get praying.

Study Guide, Day 26

In addition to praying generally as Jesus directed, and specifically for individuals, we can look to Paul's letters for guidance in praying for missionaries, since he was a missionary. What did he ask people to pray about for him? We've looked at Colossians 4:2-3. Let's take a look at verses 3 and 4 from the New International Version:

And pray for us, too, that God may open a door for our message, so that we may proclaim the mystery of Christ, for which I am in chains. Pray that I may proclaim it clearly, as I should.

What are the two things Paul asks people to pray about here?

_____

_____

_____

_____

_____

He has two requests in Ephesians 6:19-20 (NIV) as well: *Pray also for me, that whenever I speak, words may be given me so that I will fearlessly make known the mystery of the gospel, for which I am an ambassador in chains. Pray that I may declare it fearlessly, as I should.* What are they?

_____

_____

_____

_____

What are his two requests in 2 Thessalonians 3:1-2 (NIV)? *As for other matters, brothers and sisters, pray for us that the message of the Lord may spread rapidly and be honored, just as it was with you. And pray that we may be delivered from wicked and evil people, for not everyone has faith.*

_____

_____

_____

_____

_____

Are these prayer requests relevant today? How would you put those together in a prayer?

_____

_____

_____

_____

_____

Day 27: Praying as we ought

"But you shall receive power when the Holy Spirit has come upon you; and you shall be witnesses to Me in Jerusalem, and in all Judea and Samaria, and to the end of the earth." Acts 1:8

Praying for yourself might seem very strange to you right now. You may never before have thought about yourself in terms of what God has called all of us to do—to make disciples of all nations, and to pray for laborers.

The key thing this tells us is that we need to be involved in these efforts. Perhaps even more involved than you realize.

When Jesus spoke to His followers about where they would be witnesses, He didn't put a priority on one place over another. The way Acts 1:8 is phrased, Jerusalem, Judea, Samaria and the end of the earth have equal priority.

So even though I spend each day focused on making disciples at the end of the earth, I can't stop there. I also need to be vitally involved in my local church.

Now take a look around you. You should be part of a local church, and involved there.

115

You should also be involved as an ambassador of Christ in your own community. It's likely that the bulk of your praying, giving and going is local.

How well are you doing at the end of the earth? Jesus gave it equal priority. Yet I've heard it said that more than 95 percent of all the Christian workers and more than 95 percent of all the money given to God never make it out of the local context.

Pray that God shows you how He wants you to put more priority on His work at the end of the earth.

Study Guide, Day 27

Acts 1:8 tells us we will be witnesses *"in Jerusalem, and in all Judea and Samaria, and to the end of the earth."* Here are two other ways the Great Commission is stated:

Go therefore and make disciples of all the nations … (Matthew 28:19)

He said to them, "Go into all the world and preach the gospel to all creation." (Mark 16:15, NIV)

The word in Matthew translated "nations" literally means all people groups. So the call is to make available abundant, eternal life in Christ to everyone, everywhere. And more — the call is to make disciples.

Where do you think your local church fits into that? Is that part of "everyone, everywhere"? How is your local church making disciples?

_____

_____

_____

_____

_____

If you believe God wants you to increase your involvement outside of your church, does that mean He's asking you to be less involved in your church? Could He be asking for more involvement in His work overall? Or perhaps even for you to be more involved in your church?

_____

_____

_____

_____

_____

If the call is to go to everyone, everywhere, and make disciples, is there a wrong place to go? Paul wrote in Romans 15:20, *"And so I have made it my aim to preach the gospel, not where Christ was named, lest I should build on another man's foundation."* What do you think of putting a priority, as Paul did, on places where there were few or no believers?

_____

_____

_____

_____

_____

Day 28: Strength for the journey

But I have prayed for you, that your faith should not fail; and when you have returned to Me, strengthen your brethren. Luke 22:32

Faith is one of the most important building blocks in obedience.

And fear is one of the biggest stumbling blocks to obedience.

Funny how that works, isn't it?

God has been preparing you for the next step. He has been at work in your life to ensure that you are equipped for whatever He has for you now. You have the faith necessary for that.

But instead of focusing on the next step, we try to look too far ahead. We can't really tell what's up there, and it's frightening. So sometimes we choose to stop.

Yesterday's prayer—asking God to show you how He wants you to start balancing your priorities to make them His—may have put you in a spot.

Maybe He's talking to you about making more time to pray, and you don't know where to find that time. Perhaps He's asked you to give more than you think you can carve out of your budget. Or it could be that He's showing you people you need to take the gospel to, whether they are near or far.

Take a deep breath, and let's pray.

Ask God for His peace. Ask Him for that calm that comes even in difficult times because you know you're following Him. Ask Him to simply show you the next step, and to help you focus on that next step. Ask Him for the strength to take it, and the faith to trust Him with what comes next.

Praying with God | Praying for believers | Praying for self

Study Guide, Day 28

At times I really wish Psalm 119:105 read, "Your word is a GPS mapping app on my smartphone, with every turn planned out, and alternative courses ready if I miss a turn or make a detour. Oh, and highlights of where I can find the cheapest gas and the best road food and a good place to stay each night."

But it doesn't. It says: *Your word is a lamp to my feet and a light to my path.* That's the light you need for only the next step. What do you think is your next step?

_____

_____

_____

_____

Why is it not important where you think that next step is leading, or how frightening this path seems?

_____

_____

_____

_____

What do you need from God to make that next step? Can you see ways He has been preparing you? Do you need courage, strength or wisdom, or all three?

_____

_____

_____

_____

Sometimes we agonize over the next step. Perhaps there are two or more different choices. Maybe you see a couple of good steps, and are not sure what order they should be in. Do you think that God will bless you for endeavoring to move forward with Him? Do you think that God can correct your course if you're talking with Him and listening and reading His Word? Do you think you need to step out and trust Him? Do you believe God will give you wisdom to follow Him if you ask? What are you allowing to hinder you from following God's will in your life?

_____

_____

_____

_____

Day 29: Putting it all together

Rejoice always, pray without ceasing, in everything give thanks; for this is the will of God in Christ Jesus for you. 1 Thessalonians 5:16-18

One of our NTM missionaries once told me that the first time he asked a new believer to pray, the man walked up to a log and put his foot up. Then he rested his elbow on his knee, and bowed his head to rest on his hand, before he began.

That was the way the missionary had always stood while praying with them. The man was simply modeling what he'd seen. But what if there hadn't been a log handy?

Don't let the form of prayer get in the way of prayer.

Jesus told us not to pray like the Pharisees, and to go into a closet to pray (Matthew 6). His point was that we shouldn't make a show of it. Our prayers are supposed to humble us before God, not exalt us before men. Jesus often used hyperbole—or to put it another way, exaggeration as a figure of speech. He would over-emphasize something to make a point.

We don't have to pray in a closet. We can pray anywhere and everywhere. At the same time, it's important to make time alone with the Father. Luke 5:16 tells that Jesus *"often withdrew into the wilderness and prayed."*

Now, what Paul might be telling us when he writes "pray without ceasing" is that we ought not put a time limit on prayer or reduce it to a formula. Don't misunderstand me: aiming for a certain amount of time, or using a formula to help you remember to thank God and praise Him can be a good thing. Just don't let it limit you.

But I think Paul means something much deeper. How can we pray without ceasing? By coming back to the essence of prayer. It's communicating with God. We need to keep ourselves in a state of listening to God and speaking to Him. And Paul tells us how to keep those lines open: Rejoice always, and keep giving thanks. Worship Him with a grateful heart, continually.

It takes practice. And practice starts with doing it now. Let's pray.

Study Guide, Day 29

At the end of his first letter to the Thessalonians, Paul gives rapid-fire instructions:

Now we exhort you, brethren, warn those who are unruly, comfort the fainthearted, uphold the weak, be patient with all. See that no one renders evil for evil to anyone, but always pursue what is good both for yourselves and for all. Rejoice always, pray without ceasing, in everything give thanks; for this is the will of God in Christ Jesus for you. Do not quench the Spirit. Do not despise prophecies. Test all things; hold fast what is good. Abstain from every form of evil. (1 Thessalonians 5:14-22)

I can picture the Thessalonians hearing this letter read in church. "Hold on," someone might have shouted. "Slow down! Read that again!" Let's focus on what he wrote on prayer:

"Rejoice always, pray without ceasing, in everything give thanks; for this is the will of God in Christ Jesus for you."

"Pray without ceasing" is not presented as simply a good idea, but as God's will for you and for me. And it doesn't stand alone. It's sandwiched between rejoicing and gratitude.

What does "rejoice" mean to you? How is always rejoicing part of God's will?

_____

_____

_____

_____

_____

What does it mean to give thanks in everything? How is that God's will?

_____

_____

_____

_____

_____

What attitude of the heart is God's will for us? How is this attitude important to praying without ceasing?

_____

_____

_____

_____

_____

Wrapping it all up

Day 30: The circle of eternal life

"For My thoughts are not your thoughts, nor are your ways My ways," says the Lord. Isaiah 55:8

Chicago is one of my favorite cities. And in Chicago I love to go to the Art Institute, head to the Impressionists, and walk around in front of the paintings by Claude Monet.

I look at the paintings from a distance, and marvel at the way the scenes seem alive and real in a way that a photograph simply cannot capture. Then I get closer, and I cannot help but smile and shake my head.

Close, I can see that what looked like a green tree from a distance is actually composed of a variety of colors. It's not just shades of green. There may be lavender, pink and burgundy, and mustard or gold. I cannot for the life of me understand how Monet chose those colors, let alone how he decided how much of each to put where. But I admire the results.

Perhaps we need to step back a little when we are looking at God's results, too.

Up close, the results of our obedience may look like an angry splotch of red. It may seem completely out of place. Yet with a little perspective, we may realize it is a highlight on a shining breastplate of righteousness.

We may never achieve that perspective this side of Heaven. In fact, I am certain we will not be able to fully comprehend the beautiful masterpiece God is painting until we are with Him there. So we need to learn to trust Him for the results of our obedience.

We also need to learn to see beyond ourselves. We need to see, first and foremost, God. God is the One who can answer our prayers, the only One who can change our circumstances. But then we begin to realize it's really about changing us.

Seeing beyond ourselves brings the whole community of believers into focus. And as we pray for them, and love them, we are part of God's plan to unify His people. And His people can, together, reach out beyond themselves, even to the whole world.

Pray that God sends out laborers into His harvest.

Study Guide, Day 30

I'm a big proponent of looking at Scripture in context. And we can learn a great deal by looking at Matthew 28:19 as well the verses that surround it. In this case, specifically verses 18 and 20:

And Jesus came and spoke to them, saying, "All authority has been given to Me in heaven and on earth. Go therefore and make disciples of all the nations, baptizing them in the name of the Father and of the Son and of the Holy Spirit, teaching them to observe all things that I have commanded you; and lo, I am with you always, even to the end of the age."

What's the basis of Jesus' command to make disciples of all nations? Or to put it another way, why does verse 19 say "therefore"?

_____

_____

_____

_____

_____

Grammatically, "make disciples" is the active verb. But what three other actions are part of the command? How do these fit together?

_____

_____

_____

_____

_____

What promise does Jesus make to his disciples? Why is that important in this passage?

_____

_____

_____

_____

_____

What encouragement to be part of God's Great Commission do you take away from this study?

_____

_____

_____

_____

_____

Next steps

Don't stop praying and seeking God in His Word. If you stumble, get back up and keep going.

Your own church is your starting point for the next step in your journey, and if you don't have one, find one. There is no substitute for the church's role in the believer's life, or for the role of the believer in the church.

Look for opportunities to grow and to serve. Talk with your church leaders about your next steps. Listen to the guidance of wise believers. Develop and deepen relationships.

I also encourage you to look into New Tribes Mission. Our website, **ntm.org**, is a great starting point. And if you turn the page, you'll learn more about how you can get involved through New Tribes Mission.

Finally, if this book has blessed you, or I can help you move ahead in your walk with Christ, please let me know. Thank you for investing time and effort to work through this.

Ian Fallis
ian_fallis@ntm.org

About New Tribes Mission

Around the world, God is at work.

Every 45 days, New Tribes Mission reaches another people group.

Bibles are translated. Lives transformed. Churches established.

The new life God has given tribal men and women and children radiates through their own villages and even to other people groups.

God is inviting YOU. YOU can help expand the reach of the Gospel.

ntm.org/pray ntm.org/give ntm.org/go

Believers from more than three dozen countries serve together in Africa, Latin America and the Asia-Pacific region.

Working in the people's own culture and language reaches hearts and transforms lives.

Chronological Bible lessons lay a foundation so people with no concept of God can understand His redemptive plan, from creation to Christ, and then grow into mature believers.

Training is vital. Two to four years of pre-field instruction provide the basis for cross-cultural ministry. Ongoing training prepares church planters for each new challenge.

The goal is establish maturing churches. Guided by clear criteria and experienced church planters, NTM workers equip leaders and teachers, develop ongoing literacy and Bible lessons, and cultivate a body of growing believers.

Thousands of people groups—millions of men, women and children—are still waiting to hear the gospel.

Today, YOU can get involved in God's work among unreached people groups ...

ntm.org/pray   ntm.org/give   ntm.org/go

About the author

After fifteen years writing and editing at daily newspapers in Southern California, Ian Fallis and his wife, Julie, joined New Tribes Mission. They serve at the mission's USA home office in Sanford, Florida. Ian has spent the last fifteen-plus years writing about and visiting remote villages and hamlets in the Asia-Pacific region, Latin America and Africa.

Find out more about his ministry at his NTM blog, **blogs.ntm.org/ian-fallis**

Ian is also the author of several fiction novels. You can learn more about his fiction writing at his author blog, **ian-fallis.com**